JEREMY NICHOLAS was a Wolf Cub and went to Sunday School as a small boy. He became a Queen's Scout and won the Duke of Edinburgh's Gold Award. Curiously, his school reports failed to reflect any enthusiasm for these achievements, dwelling exclusively on his table manners ("leave something to be desired") his disruptive influence in the classroom ("he has been a great trial to Miss Smith") and his lack of ability to take anything seriously ("he must apply himself with vigour if he is to succeed in *any* examination"): clear indications of why he has become an actor, writer, composer and lyricist. This is his first book for delinquents.

JON ATLAS HIGHAM was one of teacher's pets at school (Oundle) – a goody-goody, a swot and a prefect. Having thus reached the acme of his ambition, he reluctantly left school and, since graduating from the Norwich School of Art, has fallen on hard times, reduced to illustrating books and painting.

RASPBERRIES AND OTHER TRIFLES

TALES FOR DISCERNING DELINQUENTS

Verses by
Jeremy Nicholas

Illustrated by Jon Atlas Higham

HUTCHINSON

London Melbourne Sydney Auckland Johannesburg

Hutchinson Children's Books Ltd

An imprint of the Hutchinson Publishing Group
17–21 Conway Street, London W1P 6JD

Hutchinson Publishing Group (Australia) Pty Ltd
PO Box 496, 16–22 Church Street, Hawthorne, Melbourne,
Victoria 3122
PO Box 151, Broadway, New South Wales 2007

Hutchinson Group (NZ) Ltd
32–34 View Road, PO Box 40-086, Glenfield, Auckland 10

Hutchinson Group (SA) Pty Ltd
PO Box 337, Bergvlei 2012, South Africa

First published 1984

Text © Jeremy Nicholas 1984

Illustrations © Jon Atlas Higham 1984

Set in Garamond by BookEns, Saffron Walden, Essex

Printed and bound in Great Britain by Anchor Brendon Ltd,
Tiptree, Essex

British Library Cataloguing in Publication Data

Nicholas, Jeremy
Raspberries and other trifles.
I. Title   II. Higham, Jon Atlas
821'.008   PR1175

ISBN 0 09 156780 7

For Mary Cecelia Willson Woolcock
on her 75th birthday

With apologies to Hilaire Belloc

The author takes a modest pride
In offering this handy guide
For children who suspect they may
Be turning both their parents grey –
Delinquents who perhaps don't know
Exactly how far they can go.
Its aim? By illustrated verse
To tempt them into doing worse.
For this, the volume is, you'll find,
The *ne plus ultra* of its kind.
Each portrait and each tale is FACT,
Though, since I am a man of tact,
The characters have been disguised
In case they might be recognized.
More pertinently, three or four
On reading this might go to law:
Incorrigible rascals who
If publicly exposed, would sue.
But never mind, I guarantee
You'll know at least *one* personally.

Contents

Gavin Clinch,

Whose life ended fruitlessly.

Of all the children I have met
The most undisciplined as yet
Was Gavin Clinch, a child of six
Who got up to all sorts of tricks.
His parents thought the world of him;
In my view this was rather dim.
They let him do just as he pleased –

He yelled,

he spat,

he burped,

he sneezed,

And didn't show the least concern –
Ah well, some parents never learn.
For (while I don't agree with caning)
Strict, relentless toilet-training
Coupled with a daily clout
Would soon have sorted Gavin out.
The folly of their lax approach
Was shown when all three went by coach
To London for the Lord Mayor's show.

Our Gavin did not want to go.
He yelled, he spat, *et cetera*,
Abused the driver and Papa,
And put his mother in a flap
By being sick near Watford Gap.

Arrived in London – what a fuss! –
They had to drag him off the bus.
Then travelled on the Underground

To Blackfriars Bridge where soon they
    found
A most convenient place to spy
The Grand Procession passing by.

His parents cheered and clapped and waved
But, oh dear, Gavin misbehaved
(No need to spell out
how
or what . . .)
Suffice to say they left the spot
And hurried to within the walls
Of Wren's magnificent St Paul's.

They thought their offspring ought to see
This shrine of English history
Where Wellington and others rest,
But Gavin Clinch was not impressed.

He ran off
down the centre aisle –
His parents lost him
for a while –
Then all at once they heard a sound
Which echoed round and round and round.

The Clinches were amazed to see
Up in the Whispering Gallery
Their son! And Gavin (oh, the shame!)
Was blowing raspberries for a game:

Not one,

not two,

not three

or four,

But eighteen, nineteen,

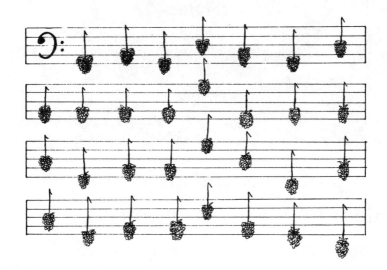

now a score.
It sounded very, *very* rude,
Quite out of keeping with the mood. . .
More like a liner leaving dock.

A group of nuns collapsed in shock,
While others tolerantly smiled,
"My *goodness*, what a noisy child!"

The scores of tourists gathered there
(And one or two had knelt in prayer)
Tut-tutted as they looked aghast
And winced at each successive blast.

The Verger wished
the Organist
Would make an effort
to resist
Such modern works,
so harsh and stark:
"Why can't he stick
to dear old Bach
And play this awful stuff
at home?"
As raspberries echoed
round the dome.
The Dean,
who heard them
from the crypt,
Rushed up the stairs
red-faced,
tight-lipped,
Suppressing thoughts
at every stride
Of imminent infanticide.

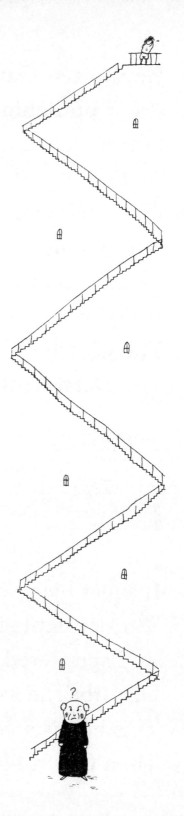

He spotted Gavin standing there,
Crept up behind him, grabbed his hair,
Frogmarched him down into the nave,
And cried, "How *dare* you misbehave!
I'll knock you
into kingdom come."
Then spanked him
soundly on the bum.
The Clinches rushed up in alarm.
The Dean held Gavin by the arm.

"Is this
your child?"
"He is,"
they said.
"And please don't cuff him round the head.
It's just high spirits, Mr Dean,"
Who mumbled something quite obscene
And spluttered, "Blowing raspberries here
Disturbs the sacred atmosphere.
This boy is a complete disgrace."
Then Gavin blew one in his face,

And ran straight out across the road,
Oblivious of the Highway Code.
He didn't look to left or right,
And – oh! it was a dreadful sight –
A ten-ton juggernaut from Dover
Couldn't stop and ran him over.

The Clinches thought it rotten luck
To have their son squashed by a truck.
The Dean consoled them, "Have you
   thought
That God might have been over-wrought,
And *had* to put his foot down here?"
"The driver did just that, I fear,"
Said Mr Clinch, who thought it odd
That juggernauts were Acts of God.

Mary-Jane and Emily,

Whose viewing habits came unstuck.

I wonder if you've been to tea
With Mary-Jane and Emily,
Twin sisters both with golden curls,
The prettiest of little girls?
They're similar in many ways –
Not least in how their tempers blaze.
At tea-time, far from eating food,
The twins are resolutely glued
To television, when they fight
For what they're going to watch that night.

They never ever can agree
Upon which programme they will see.
They pull each other's hair about
And scratch and kick and sulk and pout.
Then one day, Emily let fly –

She hit her sister in the eye
Because she wanted "Tom and Jerry".
Gracious! Her vocabulary!
Mary-Jane picked up the jelly,
Missed her sister, hit the telly.
SPLAT! It landed on the screen.
(A pity. It was tangerine.)

Unfortunately,
some of it
Ran down inside
a tiny slit
And there coagulated, which
Jammed up the programme-channel
   switch.
The telly stayed for ever more
Immovably on Channel Four.
The sisters went to see their Mum.
"Please ask the engineer to come!"
He came, he saw,
and then inquired,
"I s'pose you know
this thing is hired?
You can't throw jelly at a box!
At least, it's most unorthodox,"
A word that made the sisters gasp.
(Its meaning's *still* beyond their grasp.)
The man was really most irate
And said, "I'm going to confiscate

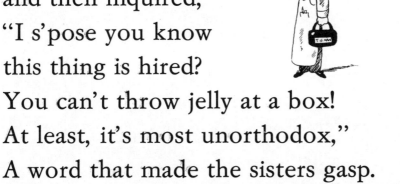

The television set right now –
This sort of thing we can't allow."
And there and then, without delay,
He took the wretched thing away.
Poor Emily and Mary-Jane
Have never had a fight again.
They have to *talk* and *read* instead,
And go *much* earlier to bed.

The moral here is plain to see:
Don't watch the box while having tea.

Quentin Courtenay-Caradine,

Who was made an offer he couldn't refuse.

A nauseating little swine
Was Quentin Courtenay-Caradine,
Who, as his name perhaps suggests,
Was one of Mother Nature's pests.

I met him when I was quite small,
A meeting I can still recall,
For from the early age of three
The lad decided he would be
The sort of chap who makes life hell

And, goodness, he succeeded well.
A bully, sadist,
snob and cad,
He was,
to put it simply,
BAD –
The sort of nasty thuggish brute

Whom
secretly
you'd like
to shoot.

He ran our class with iron rule
And terrorised the Infants' School
(A leniently run Co-ed
With trendily progressive Head
Who "spared the rod and spoiled the child".
Result? Mixed Infants running wild).

The occupants of Class 5A
Were Caradine's especial prey –

He biffed us, bashed us, blacked our
  eyes,

(The lout was more than twice our size)
He stole our homework, tweaked our
  ears,
Reducing all of us to tears.

If anybody
sneaked on him
He beat them up
behind the gym;
And if this didn't get results,
He had twin-mounted catapults –
A weapon of his own design
That brought the rebels into line.

It was a simple step from here
To be a full-blown racketeer.

He ran a small gang of his own
Along the lines of Al Capone,
Extorting from us girls and boys
Our lunch allowance, Dinky Toys,
Pet spiders, marbles, model planes

And even Hornby Dublo trains.

He pinched our crayons,

conkers and

A lot of other contraband,

Like water pistols,

bits of string,

Meccano sets

– oh, anything

From rubber balls to

sweets and nuts . . . .

We absolutely loathed his guts.
We pandered to his every whim
For in return we got from him
The promise of protection from
A Courtenay-Caradine pogrom.
No teacher ever found him out.
Of this I've not the slightest doubt,
For written on his last report
Was "Good at lessons. Good at sport.
His grasp of everything is firm.
He's had a most successful term".

.   .   .   .   .   .

Now it was thirty years before
I came across the lad once more.
I saw a headline in *The Times*:

APPALLING CATALOGUE
OF CRIMES
UNSCRUPULOUS AND VICIOUS LIES.

And there below, surprise, surprise,
The name of Courtenay-Caradine.
(It sent a shiver down my spine.)

But, oh, what bliss to see the wretch
Had earned himself a longish stretch
For burglaries and robbing banks
And other anti-social pranks.
The judge had told him that he should
Be locked up for the public good;
Which only goes to show us this:
Just how poetic justice is.

Alexander Phillinoy,

Who suffered a severe blow.

A most revolting little boy
Was Alexander Phillinoy
Who, from his very early years,
(Without tuition, it appears)
Developed with alarming zeal
A habit not at all genteel
Yet one which I must now disclose:
Young Alexander *picked his nose*,
(The subject is distasteful, yes)
And Alex did it to excess.

At breakfast time,

at lunch,

at tea,

(*Especially* in company)

Whenever *any*body looked
His thumb and finger would be hooked
Within the left- or right-hand hole;
And there he'd burrow like a mole.

He didn't care who saw him do it –
Picked it, scraped it, never blew it.
His parents did the best they could –
They smacked his hands; it did no good.
They told him it was not polite;
It was a truly *awful* sight.
They told him that a handkerchief
Was often used to bring relief
And that this small receptacle
Would help to hide the spectacle
(Which, quite apart from being rude,
Put both his parents off their food).

The more they pleaded and implored
The more young Alexander clawed
And scoured inside the dark abyss
Which was his nasal orifice.
And what was more obscene and vile
Was watching Alexander while
He *looked* at what he'd excavated,
Licked it, liked it and then ATE it.

At length his father groaned, "Enough!
Here, Alexander, take some snuff!"

He begged his son on bended knees:
"Inhale it – it will make you sneeze.
And here's a handkerchief in case
You feel the urge to wipe your face."

Young Phillinoy could not resist:
He scooped
a pile
up in his fist
And sniffed the snuff up in a trice
(A hundred grammes, to be precise).
He stuffed the lot up all at once
Accompanied by snorts and grunts.

ATCHOO!!

His father cried, "God Bless!"
And then, "Oh dear, dear! What a mess."

ATCHOO!! A-A-T-CHOO!!! And then,
  "O Lor'!"
For, red and shiny
on the floor

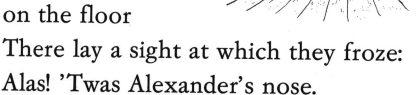

There lay a sight at which they froze:
Alas! 'Twas Alexander's nose.
His Dad gasped, "Holy Moses, son!

You had
two nostrils
– now
there's one!"
And sure enough, as black as coal,
There was, between his eyes, a hole.
· · · · · · ·

His nose is now not on his face
But in a glass museum case.
It's mounted, with a silver plate
Inscribed: 'Presented to The Tate
By Alexander Phillinoy
Who Used to Use It as a Toy.'–
A terrifying sight that's not
By any easily forgot.

Amanda Pugh,

Who became fat and famous.

AMANDA PUGH - WHO
BECAME FAT & FAMOUS

The least attractive child I knew
Was certainly Amanda Pugh.
One couldn't help observing that
She was, to put it bluntly, fat.
(Before the feminists complain,
By this, I don't mean she was plain
Or ugly in the *slightest* way.)*
Her temperament was bright and gay,
Outgoing, jolly, rarely sad,
And both her parents said she had

* In fact this is a whopping fib,
  I put it in for Womens' Lib.

A captivating smile (but which
In fact disguised a nervous twitch).
Now, while it's true that there are lots
Of pre-pubescent girls with spots,
And, even from the middle classes,
Some who wear corrective glasses;
And while *everybody* understands
When something's wrong with some-
  one's glands,
Amanda, cursed with all of these,
Succumbed to yet one *more* disease:
She over-ate. She STUFFED it in!
Her tummy was a refuse bin.

Her primary delight in life
Was sitting with a fork and knife
And eating everything in sight.

She hardly ever paused to bite –
Her mouth was like a small machine
That ploughed through Mrs Pugh's
cuisine:

Chocolates, puddings, jellies, sweets,
Lamb cutlets and all kinds of meats,
Meringues, éclairs and marzipan,
Potatoes, dumplings, strawberry flan,
Nougat, doughnuts, *pounds* of butter,

(Sometimes her Papa would mutter,
"Blimey 'Riley, girl, how can yer?"
As she crammed in more lasagne),

Guzzling baked beans, veg and fish

With double portions of each dish.
And after all this she'd implore,
"I'm hungry, Mummy! Give me MORE!"
When she'd remembered to say, 'Please,'
She'd tuck into the Stilton cheese,

The Cheddar, Brie and Camembert
And then attack the dining-chair.
(Amanda used to like to savour
Bits of wood. She loved
the flavour.)

At nine o'clock she'd go to bed
But first she'd eat a loaf of bread
And just a *little* more rice pud.
I've not met anyone who could
Dispose of so much food per day –
Not even an *adult* gourmet.

So by the time
that she was eight
She was distinctly
overweight;

To be exact, she was colossal.
A dropsical rhinoceros'll
Give you roughly the idea –
A sort of squishy-squashy sphere.

The word
they use
is 'adipose';
To me, there's
only one word:
'GROSS'.

· · · · · ·

Eventually Amanda Pugh
Left school and wondered what to do.
"I know," she thought, "I'll go and slim."
But once she'd squeezed into the gym
The people there said, "Sorry. No,
We can't reduce the *status quo*.
The fact is, sweetheart, you are fat.
You'll have to learn to live with that."
Amanda did not give up hope:
She seized hold of a long wire rope
Which had attached a heavy weight. . .
Now was this Luck? Or was it Fate?

For shortly afterwards she moved
(And both her Mum and Dad approved)
To Russia, where she changed her name
And has achieved a sort of fame.
When watching an athletics match
There's one sight you are bound to
　　catch:
Amanda Pugh, who used to be
A byword for obesity.

She's now Amanda Pughsilowa

'Peoples' Champion Hammer Thrower'.

Dominic
Formal de Hyde,

Who addressed himself to Male Rights.

Young Dominic Formal de Hyde
Was half French (on his father's side).

Like many youthful extroverts
He loved to look up ladies' skirts.

This phase is one that every boy
Appears to go through and enjoy.
Though one, I think it's fair to say,
Most people wish would go away.
For, on the whole, it disenchants
One's mother's friends and maiden aunts,
Who do not like their underwear
Subjected to a small boy's stare.

But when the time came to submerge
This normal adolescent urge,
Dominic Formal de Hyde did
Something I should call 'misguided':
He asked his mother, "Would you buy,
A summer frock for me to try?"

His mother kindly acquiesced,
And soon our Dominic was dressed
Up in an elegant chemise
That came down just below his knees.
The cut was flattering and chic,
The garment suited his physique.

His father said
he liked the dress,
Une réponse à
l'emporte-pièce!*
"*Mon Dieu*, the boy is in his teens,
Why can't he wear a shirt and jeans?
Mon fils sera une vraie risée."
Or, as an Englishman would say,
"My son will be a laughing stock."
(His father came from Languedoc.)
But Dominic ignored his scorn:
"I don't see why, when girls have worn
Men's trousers, jackets, ties and shirts
For years, men cannot put on skirts."
His Dad conceded that this view
Was, most unfortunately, true.
In fact it was beyond dispute:
His daughter wore a pin-stripe suit.

* You can't translate it, I can tell:
  I had to look it up as well.

Soon afterwards Formal de Hyde
Passed three A-levels and applied
To Oxford University
To read, yes, sociology.
His first day up, when he appeared
In floral dress, stout shoes

and beard,
Caused several students to demur,
"Is she a *him*? Is he a *her*?"
They thought it an enormous joke
To see an ordinary bloke
In such a strange mode of attire.
One wag suggested they inquire
If Dominic was on the pill.

"My God this place has gone downhill,"
The Chancellor was heard to say.
"You couldn't do this in my day."
A meeting of the Dons was called,
Who said, "Well, frankly, we're appalled.
It really is beyond the bounds
To wear these off-the-shoulder gowns.
Fetch the blighter here
and tell him
No more skirts
or we'll expel him."

So Dominic arrived to face
The learned Dons and state his case.
(He wore a frock of deep maroon
That he had bought that afternoon –
A lucky bargain off the peg
Revealing just a *hint* of leg.)
The Dean was openly impressed

And told the Chaplain, who confessed
Maroon was *very* much *his* taste.
"If I were thinner round the waist
I'd buy a purple frock today –
Whatever would the Bishop say?"
The Chancellor said, "Listen, lad.
We do not like the way you're clad.
Now, either wear your college gown
Or we shall have to send you down."

"I fail to see," cried Dominic
"Why you should think I am unique.
To wear a dress is nothing new

In Greece, in Fiji or Peru.

In Scotland it is not a crime –

An Arab wears one all the time.

And furthermore it's pretty clear
That you let lots of people here
Wear frocks and skirts, twin-sets and pearls –"
"Yes, Dominic, we call them 'girls'.
And none as yet have grown a beard;
We Dons, quite bluntly, think you're weird
And will not tolerate the view
That *haute couture* is good for you."
In short, de Hyde's defence had failed –
His days at Oxford were curtailed.

And that might well have been the end
Had Dominic not met a friend
Who offered him the perfect job
Where he could earn an honest bob.

For, through his chum, he gained
  admission
To the Equal Rights Commission –
A place where no one could care less
About the way employees dress.
Here, Dominic Formal de Hyde
Pronounces judgements that decide
When men and women are the same
(At least, I think that that's the aim).
So while he listens to the pleas
For equal opportunities
And equal pay and equal rights,
He wears his frock, his beard *and* tights.

William Winston
Edward Rose,

Who did exactly that.

William Winston Edward Rose
Is definitely one of those
Who

by the happy chance of birth,
Are pre-ordained to rule the earth.

He knew this as a tiny boy.
His great-grandad

                        (the last Viceroy
Of some long-gone Protectorate)
Became a Minister of State
                        And then,
                        amidst
                        the Nation's Cheers,

Ascended to the House of Peers –
Since when the Roses all have been
Advisors to the King or Queen.

So William Rose
(the youngest son
Of Geoffrey,
Viscount Chadlington)
Despite his lack of attributes,
Was sent to Eton, banked at Coutts,
And next was handed on a plate
A London house, a huge estate,

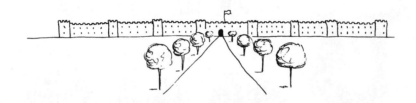

And, after scouring *Country Life*,
The dowry of his pretty wife
(A wealthy and attractive girl,
The daughter of an aged earl).
A trust fund set up by his Pa
Was registered in Panama
Which hid his income from the view
Of HM Inland Revenue.

That's how he qualified to be
A good Conservative MP,

And now he's in the Cabinet
Demanding blood, toil, tears and sweat.
"Hard work," he says, "is what we need
Before we're able to succeed.
Not one of us can live today
Unless we *work* to pay our way."

Munroe McFitt,

Who had lots of money but no fun.

The miserly McFitts reside
Near Helensburgh on the Clyde.

'The Garth' is their detached abode,
In fact it's some way from the road—
Forbidding, massive and austere.
The gates announce: GUARD DOGS
    LIVE HERE.

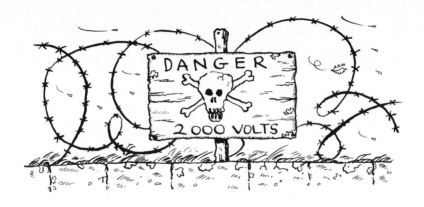

Surrounded by a twelve-foot fence
Electrified for self-defence,
'The Garth' was obviously designed
With frugal, feudal life in mind –
A cavernous and draughty pile
In pseudo-medieval style.*

* Its architect took one look, cried
And then committed suicide.

Ten bedrooms all with bath *en suite*,
Without the slightest bit of heat,

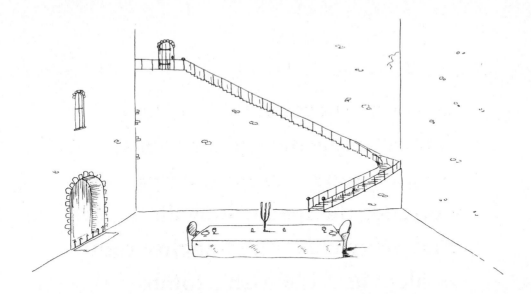

A dining hall, two kitchens and

Some furniture (all second-hand)

Combine successfully to give
A most unpleasant place to live.
An atmosphere of grim despair
Pervades the melancholy air
And every cold and draughty room
Is silent as a Pharoah's tomb.

The postman treats it with respect
And few there are who would elect
To go within a mile of it.
For inside lives

Munroe McFitt.
He made a fortune out of shipping,
Sacking men and asset-stripping.
He's got more money than Fort Knox
But wouldn't give you chicken-pox –

To get some money out of him
You'd have to tear him limb from limb.
He's stingy, niggardly and mean,
And so's his ghastly wife Eileen.

She also is immensely rich –
Descended from the Second Witch
Who met Macbeth in Shakespeare's play
(At least that's what the locals say).

They haven't got a lot of chums:
The Procurator Fiscal comes
To play the bagpipes once a year –
He used to be McFitt's cashier –
Strathspeys and reels, that sort of thing:
A somewhat gloomy Highland Fling.
This annual treat for the McFitts,
Thrills the pair of them to bits.
The pipes are all Munroe enjoys.
Apart from this distressing noise
He doesn't get much out of life
And *certainly* not from his wife.

He counts his money all alone –
No carpets, curtains, hi-fi, 'phone,
Or ornaments and pictures which
Might indicate that he was rich.
A suit of armour, brown with rust,
A stuffed hyena, thick with dust,
Inherited from his Papa
Are all the *objets d'art* there are.
McFitt's a misanthropic man –
I'm glad *I'm* not one of his clan.

Peter Popinjay,

Who pestered pets and prospered.

To love our furred and feathered friends
Is something everyone commends.
However, Peter Popinjay
Is not disposed to feel this way.
To him, the only bird or beast
He likes is one that is deceased.

· · · · · ·

It started when the lad was two;
His Mummy
took him
to the zoo
To see the sea-lions for a treat –
She thought they would amuse young Pete.
Unfortunately for the pair,
A llama who was living there
Caught sight of Peter and his Mum
And, being somewhat troublesome,
He showed, by spitting llama phlegm,

Exactly what he thought of them.
The llama's unprovoked attack
Quite took the little lad aback
(And, frankly, one can sympathise –
It got him right between the eyes.)

From then on every vertebrate
Became the object of his hate.
He started off with bugs and flies:
Oblivious to their insect cries
He pulled their legs off one by one
And found it was enormous fun.

Progressing rapidly
to things
That flew with somewhat larger wings,

 He shot down
every passing
sparrow
With his homemade bow-and-arrow.
His Dad exclaimed, "Cor, stone the crows!"
Said Pete, "That's just what I propose,"
And picking up a nearby brick
He muttered, "This should do the trick."
Soon afterwards his parents saw
A sight that shook them to the core.
Their son had put inside a jar
The family's
pet budgerigar.
He'd screwed the lid down tightly so
The budgie couldn't say 'Hello'.
"You mustn't do that, Pete," they said,
But by that time the bird was dead.
The next to suffer was the cat.

It made a useful cricket bat,

A handy ball,

a pair of stumps . . .

It came up in all sorts of lumps.

Three overs later, it retired

And shortly after that expired.

His first report from school read: "He
Is brilliant at biology.
The boy is keen and quick to learn."
But soon this took a nasty turn –
A most unhealthy predilection
For the classes in dissection.
Cutting up
dead frogs
and cats,
Examining the spleens of bats
Is standard practice, it's the norm . . .

 But not
without some
chloroform.

The teachers started taking bets
On why so many pupils' pets
Mysteriously went astray –
They smelt a rat, as one might say.

The odds on Popinjay were short;
Inevitably he was caught.
And what they found was quite grotesque,
For there, concealed inside his desk,
Were parts of the anatomy
Of several pets that used to be –

A skull, a scalpel, and some fur . . .
They fetched the Head.

"Excuse me, sir –
Alert the RSPCA.
We've found the culprit – Popinjay."
He was a murderous little bod,
A teeny-weeny Sweeney Todd.

·   ·   ·   ·   ·   ·

Eventually he grew to be
A pillar of society –
A businessman of great renown
With interests in every town.
When next you pass a butcher's shop
And see some mincemeat or a chop

Remember Mr Popinjay
For he's provided the display.
His line of trade is wholesale meat
And every bit is killed by Pete:
He runs his abattoir with pride
And flogs the stuff off nationwide.
Yes, Peter Popinjay it is who
Caters for your joint or stew,
Your bacon, sausages and suet.
(Heavens! *Someone*'s got to do it!)

He's tried to get permission to
Sell llama cutlets from the zoo

But no one there will let him harm a
Cuddly, lovely, little llama.

Still, every week he goes to see
The llama in captivity;
Each week he brings a sharpened knife
And swears, "I'll have that llama's life."
And every week it is the same;
The llama treats it as a game:
It catches sight of him, then waits,
And, when in range, expectorates.

Cynthia Simpson,

Who stuck it out to a bitter end.

A habit that is commonplace is
Pulling lots of silly faces.
Cynthia Simpson found that she
Could do this most amusingly.

For once, when she was very young,
She found, by sticking out her tongue,
It did not only look quite rude, it
Was so long that it extruded
Right up to her nose's tip
(So handy, when it chanced to drip)
And down to just below her chin.
She hardly ever kept it in
But stuck it out at everyone –
Her school friends thought it *heaps* of fun.

She'd screw her face up, go cross-eyed
And wag her tongue from side to side,
Then hunch her back, and strike a pose,
Blow out her cheeks and lick her nose,
Or wave her hands and squint and leer
And make her eyeballs disappear –

A kind of facial acrobat.
Her Dad said,

               "It will stick like that.
You mark my words." "Oh phooey, Dad,"
Said Cynthia. But, next day, it had.
If only she had said "Okay"
She wouldn't have a lisp today.
She findth it hard to thay her name.
Her tongue thtickth out. Itth thuch a shame.
She altho hath to wear a bwathe
To keep pwotwuding teeth in plathe,
And whatth an even gweater pity –
Thynthia thtarted out quite pwetty.

95